Armor

Catriona Clarke

Designed by Tom Lalonde

Illustrated by Terry McKenna

Armor consultant: Bridget Clifford,
Senior Curator, Royal Armouries, HM Tower of London

Reading consultant: Alison Kelly, Roehampton University

Contents

What is armor?

Soldiers wore armor to
protect them when
they were fighting.

This is a copy of
a helmet that
was made over
1,000 years ago.

A helmet like
this protected
a soldier's head,
neck and face.

3

Hard wear

Many people think of knights in shining armor, but knights weren't the only ones who wore protection in battle.

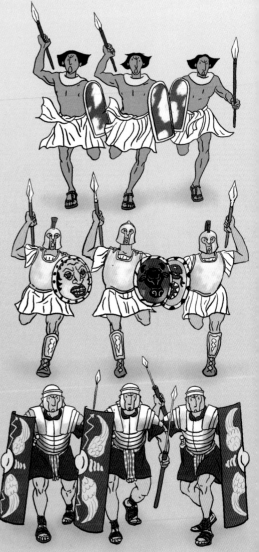

In Ancient Egypt, most soldiers just carried shields to protect themselves.

The Ancient Greeks wore helmets, and metal plates on their chests and legs.

Roman soldiers wore body armor made from lots of strips of metal.

The Japanese warrior in this old painting
is wearing armor made from leather,
metal and silk.

Lots of links

A thousand years ago, knights wore armor that was made from tiny metal rings. This was called mail.

A mailmaker made thousands of rings from a strong metal called iron.

It was easy to move around and fight in mail.

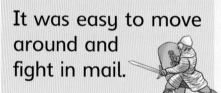

Then he linked the rings together in lots of rows to make a mail shirt.

The knight wore the shirt and a mail hood. He wore a helmet, too.

The old tapestry below shows knights wearing mail during a battle.

Wicked weapons

Mail was good, but it couldn't protect a knight against all of the weapons he had to face.

Archers shot arrows that went through mail armor.

Clubs called maces hurt knights, even though they didn't break their mail.

Soldiers often used halberds to hook enemy knights from their horses.

These men are dressed up as knights. They are wearing mail and carrying long weapons called lances.

Slashing swords

Swords were made from strong metal. The best swords could cut through mail armor.

The knights in this old painting are attacking each other with swords.

In battle, a knight used his sword to slash and hack at enemy knights.

He also used the point of his sword to stab through gaps in his enemy's mail.

In an emergency, he could hold the sword's blade and swing it like a club.

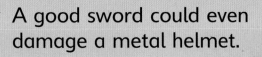

A good sword could even damage a metal helmet.

Plating up

A new type of armor was invented to give knights better protection than mail. It was called plate armor.

A helmet protected the face and head.

The knight's chest was protected by a breastplate.

The knight's knees were protected by poleyns.

The metal shoes were called sabatons.

Gauntlets protected the hands and wrists.

Knights wearing plate armor were much safer from maces and arrows.

Hard hats

A knight's helmet was a very important part of his armor as it protected his head.

Helmets with rounded tops were best. Swords and arrows bounced off them more easily.

A knight usually wore a padded cap under his helmet to make it fit better.

Some helmets had a visor that a knight could pull down to protect his face.

Many visors had lots of little holes, so it was easier for the knight to breathe.

A visor protected a knight's face, but he couldn't see very much through the eye slits!

Making armor

Plate armor was very expensive. It took lots of people to make each suit of armor.

1. Sheets of metal were hammered into the right shape for each piece of armor.

2. The pieces were polished on a wheel until they were really shiny.

3. A locksmith made the buckles and hinges that fastened the armor together.

4. The armor was put together to check that all the pieces fit properly.

The best armor was tested with a crossbow and arrow to check that it was strong enough.

Some knights' horses had armor made for them too.

Getting dressed

Every knight had a young squire to help him get ready for battle.

The squire made sure that the knight's horse was ready to ride.

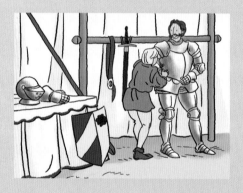

He helped the knight to get dressed and to put his suit of armor on.

The squire helped the knight onto his horse and then gave him his weapons.

The knight in this old painting is saying goodbye to his family before he rides into battle.

In battle, a knight could get very, very hot inside his armor.

Coats of arms

Knights carried shields made of wood. These were good for protection, but they also showed who was who in a battle.

When knights wore helmets, it was hard to tell who they were fighting...

...so each knight had a pattern called a coat of arms painted onto his shield.

Sometimes a knight's horse wore his coat of arms too.

Some of the coats of arms had special meanings. The lions on these shields mean bravery.

Boys to men

It wasn't easy to become a knight. There was lots to learn and it took a long time.

Very young boys used wooden swords to learn how to fight.

Older boys became squires. They did jobs for knights.

Squires practiced their skills using real swords and armor.

They also practiced riding and aiming a lance at a target.

Boys sometimes danced in their armor to get used to its weight.

When a squire was old enough, he became a knight in a special ceremony.

This old picture shows a king about to knight a squire.

Joust!

A joust was a contest between two knights. Each knight tried to knock the other one off his horse.

Jousting knights wore extra strong armor that was very heavy.

A knight rested his lance on his special jousting shield.

Some knights carried special shields that exploded to make the joust look more exciting.

He lowered his head to see through the slit in his visor...

... then lifted his head up at the last minute to protect his eyes.

Fighting fashion

Some knights liked to wear very fancy armor with lots of decoration.

Armor like this was only worn in parades. It was not strong enough for fighting.

Beautiful patterns could be added to suits of armor.

Sometimes armor was made to look just like clothes.

Knights sometimes had armor painted with a coat of arms.

Helmets were decorated with gold and feathers.

Some helmets were made in the shape of animal heads.

End of an era

A new weapon was invented about 500 years ago. It was called the gun.

Armor had to be made very thick and strong to protect against bullets...

... but this made it much more difficult to move around and fight in.

Lots of knights decided not to bother wearing armor any more.

This picture was painted just after guns
were invented, when the age of armor
was coming to an end.

Glossary of armor words

Here are some of the words in this book you might not know. This page tells you what they mean.

 knight - a soldier who rode a horse. Knights wore armor for protection.

 mail - armor made up of thousands of tiny metal rings.

 plate armor - armor made from sheets of metal.

 gauntlets - metal gloves to protect a knight's hands.

 poleyns - curved pieces of armor to protect a knight's knees.

 sabatons - metal shoes worn by knights to protect their feet.

 coat of arms - a picture on a shield. Every knight had his own coat of arms.

Websites to visit

If you have a computer, you can find out more about armor on the Internet. On the Usborne Quicklinks Website there are links to four fun websites.

Website 1 - Dress a knight in his armor.

Website 2 - Look at photos of weapons and armor.

Website 3 - Design your own coat of arms.

Website 4 - Try an exciting joust game.

To visit these websites, go to **www.usborne-quicklinks.com** Read the Internet safety guidelines, and then type the keywords "beginners armor".

The websites are regularly reviewed and the links in Usborne Quicklinks are updated. However, Usborne Publishing is not responsible, and does not accept liability, for the content or availability of any website other than its own. We recommend that children are supervised while on the Internet.

Index

Acknowledgements

Photographic manipulation by Nick Wakeford and John Russell
Americanization by Carrie Armstrong

Photo credits

The publishers are grateful to the following for permission to reproduce material:
© akg-images, London 26; © The Board of Trustees of the Armouries 12-13, 17; © The Bridgeman Art Library/Getty Images 6-7; © British Library 19 (Harley MS 4431, f.135), 29 (Burney MS 169, f.21v); © Clive Hawkins 1, 24-25; © CORBIS 10 (The Archivo Iconografico, S.A.), 23 (The Art Archive), cover (Darama), 21 (Gianni Dagli Orti), 14 (Nik Wheeler), 5 (Sakamoto Photo Research Laboratory); © Photolibrary.com 8-9; © The Royal Armouries/HIP/TopFoto 31; © The Trustees of the British Museum 2-3.